Where the Leaves Darken

WHERE THE LEAVES DARKEN

A Collection of Poems By

STEVEN PELCMAN

BOOKS

Adelaide Books
New York / Lisbon

2018

Where the Leaves Darken
A Collection of Poems
By Steven Pelcman

Copyright © 2018 By Steven Pelcman
Cover Image © 2018 Steven Pelcman

Published by Adelaide Books, New York / Lisbon

Cover design & Interior Formatting:
Adelaide Books DBA, New York

Editor-in-Chief
Stevan V. Nikolic

All rights reserved. No part of this book may be reproduced in any manner whatsoever without written permission from the author except in the case of brief quotations embodied in critical articles and reviews.

For any information, please contact Adelaide Books
at info@adelaidebooks.org
or write to
Adelaide Books
244 Fifth Avenue, Suite D27
New York, NY, 10001

ISBN13: 978-1-7320742-6-2
ISBN10: 1-7320742-6-7

Printed in the United States of America

Dedicated to Mom and Dad
And to Lola

The road is worn
By shades of light
Until we reach a spot
Where the leaves darken

Steven Pelcman

WILD ROSE
(For Lola)

As a sweet goddess
you run your perfume
with gentle wind.

Mother of queen bee
and victim of hand
and heart, you spread

your wings as a seasoned
veteran and summer virgin
in prayer that sits

in judgment flowering
of dark red among wild green
to become the purest lover

that breathes life and death
and dares autumn
to keep summer in its breast.

Steven Pelcman

Contents

Summer in the Catskills   *13*
Velvet: A Cocker Spaniel's Story   *16*
A Tree Speaks Out in Winter   *18*
Sunday Morning on Madeira   *19*
Bird Song   *21*
In New Orleans, an Old Black Man Tells You about the South   *22*
Pilgrimage Ends at Fatima   *24*
A Hospital View   *26*
Voices   *27*
Sunrise over La Gomera   *28*
An Ending   *31*
My Father's Bicycle   *33*
Sea Lions on California Coast   *35*
An Irish Voice   *37*
Teenage Mother   *38*
First Morning Tram   *40*
Chapel of Bones   *42*
Homeless   *43*

44 Last Visit
45 Notes from Eastern Germany
46 Oma and Her Cat
47 The Last Time I Saw My Sister
49 Painting of Witnesses on the Road to the Crucifixion
50 Jerusalem
54 Under the Pantheon in Paris Where the Righteous are Buried
56 The Color of History Will Break Your Heart
59 New Year's Day in Prague
61 The Waiting
62 A Cup of Tea
63 Old Man Walking to Market Place in Early Spring
64 Giverny
65 Easter Spring Walk
67 Meditation
68 Cats
70 A Tourist's Welcome

Florida Turkeys Running Wild *72*

Fishing on the Galata Bridge *74*

Remembering Marrakech *76*

Sidewalk Bakery *78*

Lorelei *80*

A Quiet, Lonely Room for Dying *82*

Concentration Camp Number 144988 *84*

The Last Train to Auschwitz *86*

A Father's Last Seven Days *88*

Anne Frank Speaks *91*

Looking Down while Walking *93*

Waiting at Night *95*

A Proper Place *97*

A Mother's Final Journey *98*

A Father Leaving *100*

Madrid *103*

Hailfingen-Tailfingen 1944-45 *105*

Toulouse *107*

109   The World Beneath

111   A Giraffe Surprises Us

113   Spring

115   Every Season

117   Keystone Cowboy

119   Three Graves

121   A Sad Tune

123   About the Author

125   Publishing Credits

Summer in the Catskills

Once home was the smell
of wild strawberries
gloating on bushes
changing the summer air

in a tangled circus
of ancient trees
behind the small bungalow
we stayed in each summer.

I refused to hold
my sister's hand
as we skipped
and shuffled

along the dirt paths
of the circled rim
of forest that deer
poke their heads through

in the golden ring
of darkness that settled
above us in the musty
wooden coolness.

The dark was darker then
and as the sun stirred
the air baby-red,
the knotty pine that drifted

Steven Pelcman

my way scared me
with its carnival masks
and new-born distortions
and earthy silence.

My sister was
oblivious to the wind,
to the encroaching breathing
not our own

to the sounds
we thought we heard
of running water
over polished stone

as she held onto me
in the darkness
I could barely touch
or see through.

We began to run
through cobwebs
and clouds of mosquitoes
that hung in the air

dropping our mother's bowl
of strawberries
bleeding over dry leaves
and caked mud

until we reached
the backside of the bungalow's
slant boards and spidery windows
out of breath.

We wondered if forests
talk to other children
or if it was a secret
all our own.

Steven Pelcman

Velvet: A Cocker Spaniel's Story

Cheri says the kids like to play
outside in the countryside
of upstate New York

where the occasional criminal
is a black bear
tossing aside garbage cans

or a deer darting
in and out of the wood
that surrounds the property.

But Velvet always accompanies
Deanna and Justin as she rolls
in the first dreams of early

sunlit mornings turning green patches
of grass where the leaves
darken into pools of memory and bone.

She runs, knowing the land
is thick with hills and forest
and where its secret hiding places

are as Cheri rides the tractor
following the sun-sloped curve
of dog into black grass of flies

splintering to the next spot
of stillness as green stretches itself out
to change color before the trees.

Velvet ignores the machinery sounds
and bounces in the shadows
of spring swallows feeding on misplaced bugs.

Her hollow bark seems endless
and full of long-pointed
wings and dizzy flies.

When dusk light approaches
and the kids watch the sun
set behind the smoky hills

and the sky turns as dark
as Velvet's eyes,
she sits as a soft wooden moment

by Justin and Deanna's side
when dogs dream
and chase the color of grass.

Steven Pelcman

A Tree Speaks Out in Winter

There is no wind
yet my leaves fall
as if God
plucks them

one by one
and sends my brittle
wings tumbling
and cracking the air

to mummify
on the cold pavement
into corpses waiting
for rain or snow

or the simple movement of feet,
and as each part of me
shudders and whispers
before landing

you can almost hear
my body shift
its branches to one side,
and sigh.

Sunday Morning on Madeira

The morning haze lifts its veil
and church bells cling
to the rise of color in
the Angels Trumpets and Hibiscus
and the stuttering agility
of wall lizards.

Sunlight spreads across
the hills and through the odd mix
of Evergreens and Laurels, Palms
and Jacaranda and Coral beside
the stiffened green pose of bananas
and the echoes of dog barks to the sea.

It is time for the old men
who were once farmers
to meander down the hills
with their canes and brim hats,
their wives behind them,
to the cobblestone streets

of Funchal to worship
in the little church
removed from the hawkers
at the market and the tour buses
and the waiters on sidewalks
squealing out their menus

Steven Pelcman

in the aroma of the sea,
so that they can sit together
in the pews sharing the same scent of day,
praying to be rid of the African winds
and sip a glass of Poncha or look for
dolphins' jumping arc above the waves.

Bird Song

The singing of canaries
kept for the dying
warned them of gas leaks

as Opa crept through copper mines
at 15 pushing a wagon filled
with blocks of stone

clearing the way
past men, whose gaunt faces
were pierced and bloodied by stone-chips

sharing the dark heat of each other
for just moments in line
before taking their turn

in a spot rumbling
with every shoulder-throw
of the pick.

Steven Pelcman

In New Orleans, an Old Black Man
Tells You about the South

People shuffle along
Jackson Square Park
in the powdered sugar air
and stop to listen
to a man whose eyes

are closed as he sings and sweats
for the small change
in your pocket and you watch
the world swallowed up
by his voice.

From slave to street musician
the songs are the same and
when he opens his eyes
a sky of crow leads you
to a spot still dark after they are gone,

and full of the Mississippi,
lost children, lost bones,
surrounded by valleys
of cotton, magnolia
and the scent of night-moon jasmine.

The sun sets and people move
away into crowds of tourists
as pigeons dance wing to wing
circling statues and
boys tap for money

three-quarter time
against the street
in the shadows
squeezed between
sure men and slow women.

Steven Pelcman

Pilgrimage Ends at Fatima

Under the Portuguese sun
history has been worn down
by centuries and the trembling fear
of flu corpses piled
into horse drawn wagons

sandwiched and smothered
and sprinkled by holy water
to the WW1 visions of
Mary in green pastures.
They still come and plant their knees,

believing that god
nurtures the dry earth
to rise with moisture
as they drag along
the grey cement

whipping their bodies
into torn skin
sledding damaged limbs
to pilgrimage their beliefs away
towards the Basilica.

No one who watches
their shuffling does not feel
their pain, does not reverberate
with the sounds of the lash
as they move inch by inch.

Some are with sawed off
stubs for legs wearing fedoras
and handkerchiefs to wipe away
the sweat and hide the tears.
Others exert their chests

steering their knees in straight lines
while rowing themselves
in the cool mist of early summer
as gawking spectators
praying in the thousands

mumble and chant waiting to see
virgins appear in holy images
and men in black robes
bless the poor
with rosary beads.

Steven Pelcman

A Hospital View

A nurse, young and nervously
smiling and dressed in white
steps outside
for a quick cigarette

and appears from out of a cluster
of trees, pious in their withering,
and whose branches
are clasped in prayer.

As a manifestation of blackness
marching alone to God's calling
she leaves frosty breaths
in the falling snow that shields

the building, somber and pale,
as she releases small puffs
of smoke into the cold air
when she opens an umbrella

and how much alike trees they are,
even the building bearing
the weight of the moment
suffering against a pale sky.

Voices

You do not have to
tell me
how sadness can find
its way
into our hearts
or of how hard it is
to learn

to love what we love
and grow into
differences easily
the way flowers lean
towards the light
but if we hear

the voices within us
and believe that a
falling rain
or soft sunlight
against skin
like the caress of our
fingers

understands our love
with words so gentle,
then even the dying
would stop and listen.

Steven Pelcman

Sunrise over La Gomera

Whales roam the outer waves
far from the rocky cliffs
that shroud the volcanic ash.
Seagulls tip their wings
against the darkness
and cackle, then grieve

as the black sky
separates itself
from the ocean
the way lovers embracing
step backward.
What light that emerges

grows between them
as the sun rises
slowly out of sleep
and then with
the energy of a child
runs wild

so that everything
before it blurs,
but the sounds are pure,
so much that even
the trembling voices
of ocean now pushing its way

towards you,
bathes you in salt
and the memory of the Adriatic
when you had left foot prints
in the sand
but could not understand,

how they could vanish
under the white foam
that crawled as you did,
and like a thief,
steal all you had ever owned.
The sun unfolds

and reveals everything
like an open secret
and changes the color
of your eyes
and of the ancient-cold
stone walls full of

buried legends behind you
that where long ago
lovers rendezvoused
and dreamed of escape.
They are still alive
and roped in green

Steven Pelcman

with unknown flowers
for hands, on fire, and home
to the curious movement of lizards
seeking shelter in crevices.
You have always said,
you are made of water

and belong to the sea
never having known an ocean
till now, but always imagining
what lies beyond the stories
that had been read to you
as a child.

An Ending

Looking out at the last day
as it loses its breath
in the fog and mist

trees become spies
leaning over
or standing upright

against the light
below buildings
sticking out of the

grey shadows like lost
souls and strangers
unto themselves.

I used to imagine
the sea this way,
reaching out

into nothingness
knowing that what floats
beneath me is a movement

of life fuller than any dream
and as quiet as a lover's whisper
and I knew that this

is what hunger is
that in this open field
of wet tongues and silent birds

Steven Pelcman

in-between these glossy buildings
like ghosts that this
is where animals come to die.

This is where memories
return to when we have forgotten
who we are.

This is where the moon
sleeps until the sun
can return the reflections

that have slipped
away
into the dying light.

My Father's Bicycle

It was my father's bicycle
but after his death,
during late afternoon visits

I owned the earth turning
beneath us measuring the weight
the pedal could manage

and surprised by the resistance
of wind that carries his voice
with each stride.

With one pants leg rolled up
riding past colorless, aging small houses
into the similar black and white

photograph albums of after-war
pictures he used to show me
how a crippled city could so easily

expose its pain. The bicycle hums along
taking us to a place it knows best
unused to the differences that trust

forgives. Over the narrow
cobblestone streets, which feel the loss
yet guide us to the riverbank and forest

Steven Pelcman

where the embarrassed sunlight
separates the darkness and touches
each leaf before reaching its end

beneath the passing waters
drifting from view. Dangling legs
stretch out in the drowning reflections

not quite sure if it has heard
this song before.

Sea Lions on California Coast

A lonely ship
is ghostly
in the shadow

of a rocky cliff
disjointed from land
like an obscure limb

and is carried adrift
by the lilting voice
of black waves

that erupt with the hollow
growls that echo
through the fog.

Not unlike the mad, the lost,
the greedy struggling for life
they are unrecognizable figures

scurrying insanely,
waddling against jagged rocks
beating their cruel flesh

out from the sticky sea
with a raw beauty that grows
out of the sand.

Steven Pelcman

Their whiskers deep
into the blackness
of one another

the wild wind surrounds them
as they couple, bark
and wallow across slabs

of sea-stone
mating brutally into layers
of boundless lumps.

An Irish Voice

It is not uncommon
to hear a drowning voice
from a horse-mudded path
to the sea

where beyond these unruly
clumps of grass
tide-waters swallow
the shifting sand.

Only two summers before
a young woman
dared the oncoming
darkness and was taken away.

Geese know well
the high pitch
of Irish wind
which floods the bog

and runs among
the silent stones,
the tangled primrose
and daffodils in bloom.

Steven Pelcman

Teenage Mother

She sits down, suddenly,
changing the air and making
the darkness smaller

holding a baby
in her arms
but the look in her eyes

tells me this
is bigger than
the two of us

and I lean back
pushing the book
on my lap aside

thinking of this
teenage girl
as a mother

as the train rumbles
over the tracks
through the German night.

I do not want
to paint her
with the brushstrokes

of a lonely canvass
thinking someone
must be waiting for her

as the baby makes
gurgling sounds
full of tiny bubbles

and smacks her lips,
her tiny fingers
grasping at the windows

rattling and shaking
knowing the world
is out of reach.

It is impossible
to not build a story,
to not want

to save her
and keep her safe
under a glowing moon

chasing us through tunnels
and forests and city lights;
mere blurs of window reflections

as my heart beat increases
in the dim shadows
that separate us.

But what if my story
is not her story
even though you tell yourself,

in tiny whispers,
it is the only way
your life makes any sense.

Steven Pelcman

First Morning Tram

Out of a dark sleep
the tram argues its way
around the curve
full of metallic screeching

like vultures' foreplay
but it is too late
for this little finch
who must have known

the speed of things
and had measured incorrectly
although perhaps it had
misunderstood the new light

now that the season is changing.
And yet it had been
an unexpected moment
of its body surrendering

to a loss of flight
and the quiet turning
of feathers spinning away
to the sides of the rails

full of the city rumbling
in its ears.
It lies there as
a fist full of color

or a rumpled pair
of woollen socks,
the sort you see lying around
sometimes forgotten by small children,

and isn't it clear
that forever it will carry
those endless sounds
inside of its stuffed self.

Steven Pelcman

Chapel of Bones
(Evora, Portugal 1224)

The earth turned
five thousand souls out
from beneath the ground
for a new monastery to be built
so that the silence of monks

could fill the lives
of the living.
Death lingers,
for nothing but bones
meet the eye.

Skulls are organized into columns,
eye sockets are full of cobwebs
and ghostly in the camera flashes
that explode across beams
and above windows

where at every side, wedged in,
fragments of entire families
decorate the walls where black crosses
hang and bear the pain
of centuries.

Homeless

In the burnt shadows
of a doorway's porch light

a man eats a thrown away slice
of cake swallowing up the moon,

as crumbs separate into stars falling
onto the dark sidewalk.

I barely noticed the silence
of his baby girl,

her sleeping bag, a doll's face,
tucked beneath the light.

Steven Pelcman

Last Visit

Three years gone
and the shaping of her
takes forever

in the way shadows
take long in their dying
away from the light.

Lying side by side
the way animals pretend sleep,
she notices everything

and locks her sex away
before turning like an old blanket
safe in its corner.

Shifting only to the sound
of a cab waiting in February snow,
she quietly takes possession

of both pillows
to not disturb the moonlight
behind frozen glass.

Unspoken words work
their way into the sounds
of everything, and if you

listen, the world becomes smaller
when at 4 am, a honking horn
gives voice to falling snow.

Notes from Eastern Germany

There, an old round woman
on the sidewalk bent over
with measured breath,

her hands in red gloves
throws cubes of coal
through an open cellar window

into the dark
where grandchildren's small fingers
underneath the sill

become stars and moons,
playful targets that ease
the stiffness in her back.

The air is dizzy
with forced winds
from trams that pass

around her corner
of black dust and tulips
keenly aware of every movement.

Steven Pelcman

Oma (Grandmother)
and Her Cat

Oh, how Pauli on top of window sill,
full of stone's breath
and winter light,

would sniff the air
and offer approval,
to Oma's circular prance
of stiff knee and narrowed sight.

Posing for afternoon shadows
or chasing fur-ball moons
was a practice of delight

never knowing whose purpose
was served more,
Pauli's independence,
or Oma's sense of fright.

The Last Time I Saw My Sister

she was holding onto her bones
with the breath of angels
hating the white in her cheeks
for it reminded her of birth.

There was enough white
she'd say,
pinching the tight skin on her face

looking for something
to burn bright
buried in a gully
of vein and bone.

All alone
catching smiles with her teeth
she would tremble back

into the darkness
to the hospital bed
in the living room
and wait for sunlight

to fill the room
and warm
her crab-apple body

Steven Pelcman

caught in the imagination of toes
nibbling on every last moment,
she continually reminded herself
to remember

where to leave her robe,
eyeglasses and slippers.

Painting of Witnesses on the Road to the Crucifixion

The ghostly beauty
of her ruffled neck
gives birth to a fleshy darkness

that sweeps towards bodies
pressed against canvas
framed in gold.

She carries an unknown width
to her last stride
yet she is narrow at the hips

where her arms
are uncomfortable and yielding
in the dying light.

The folds of a garment
draped across the shoulders
of the veined neck

of a young soldier
wears the strange light
of a rising moon,

and the dull eye
of a lost child,
full of God and fear,

stares at Raphael's angels
lurking in corners
witnessing an endless death.

Steven Pelcman

Jerusalem

You can still hear
his slow shuffling
weighing heavily against
the cobblestones,

the deep breaths
gasping for air
as the pain
on the faces of witnesses

marvel at the long-
wooden cross he bore
made them breathe
with him.

In and out
of the early shadows
of old Jerusalem
captive to the stench

of men and spices,
where we now walk
on the same path
to prayers sung aloud

over speakers in the sunny
cool air of February
and the musical rhythm
of these prayers in a language

we do not know
but does not feel
foreign and somehow
manages to accompany the vendors

selling pita bread and olives,
yarmulkes and ice cream as old women
pass like shipwrecks darkened
against the sea

and sit huddled against a wall
bundling parsley and shielding their eyes
from cameras and the strange curiosity
they have come to expect.

The khaki green uniforms
of Israeli soldiers
and the machine guns strung
on their backs as if bringing

goods to market does not stop
the traffic pace of worshippers
speeding by when an old man
stooped and wearing a red fez

smiles as he drags smoke
from a water-pipe and then sips
tea still smiling at women buying
Christ replicas and wooden crosses.

Alleyways yield to the reverberating
sounds where rugs hang
in slaughtered meat
fashion and with each footstep

Steven Pelcman

there is a gentle reminder
of distant footsteps, of a wall
that wears little notes
tucked into its crevices

of the faithful bowing before
bricks Herod had built
of donkeys passing
and long drawn sighs

flushed with the breath of God
that had once passed this way
where the light has never changed
in the dark passageways of old Jerusalem.

Under the tunnels little Palestinian boys
play soccer near the checkpoints
where on the other side
the tiled blue façade of a mosque

sits brilliantly silent
at the Temple Mount
still living out Muhammad's
night journey

and lined by the black shadows
of women in burqas passing in
long strides against the sunlight
and whose eyes peer out

to warn you
that men pray
and leave shoes
outside the mosque door

that only if you read the
Qur'an can you enter
and if you look
directly into the sun

to the Mount of Olives
you can hear the silence
of the bones and dust
of Jews that have sat for 3,000 years

beyond the golden dome.
The shofar blows into the wind
along with the loudspeaker prayers
and the sounds of footsteps.

Steven Pelcman

Under the Pantheon in Paris
Where the Righteous are Buried

She finds herself flustered
and walking in a circle,

fidgeting as a child
on her father's lap

nervously awaiting for the stories
of old Europe to unfold.

She remembers the bedroom night-light
had burned with the romance of Paris,

with the stillness of the Seine
and the passion of shadows

as her father read aloud
while she dreamed.

As quiet as her father's footsteps
leaving the room,

she stands still in the tombstone air
underground as the filtered light

creeps into the cubicle
and changes color.

She could not help
caressing stone after stone

walking past coffins
the way wind silently

springs up and explores
every space unguarded

and fills every living thing
with its memory.

Steven Pelcman

The Color of History Will Break Your Heart

They have run from terror,
their voices parched
from the night air,
from prayer and the quiet begging

and wailing heaved all day
on the streets of Paris
as the night finds them knotted
and bundled asleep.

Set back from the street corner
under a lamppost
that captures a little child's
wide-open eyes counting moths

flying free and unafraid
in the warm light,
this family of lumpy shadows
almost ready to be measured

for freshly dug graves,
uses the darkness
to cover their bodies
and keep them safe.

It is a moment
unlike any other
as they are not used to
not dreaming, having reached

their final destination
against the cold granite headstones
of Paris buildings and yet
there is a familiarity shared

in the hopelessness and emptiness
of that little child's face,
who had to walk over mass graves
that disappeared in the dry earth

and then shudder to the sounds
of crashing waves against the brittle wood
of a ship leaning heavy to its side
and full of people clinging to the thought

that at least water does not bring pain
and cleanses the soul
so that god can forgive them
for their sins.

But here, wedged up against
the towering world
they had dreamed of
and no longer wooed

by the throaty sounds
of burros and the cold desert air,
when they first told stories
of freedom around the night fires,

they have come to accept
an ancient fate that dark voices
tell them is theirs to keep,
theirs to own, voices emanating

Steven Pelcman

from the chipped stone
of buildings they use for shelter,
stones rumbling with more
than the sounds of their own hunger

or the thundering iron of metro
and steel that penetrates the earth
under their feet and the dark destiny
for a little child who ought to be smiling

but who instead finds herself resting
upon the wandering souls
stone-deep in a labyrinth
they cannot escape

as she cannot escape
for she understands
the secret of the dying
and of sand and water and concrete.

She knows
there is no adventure
other than the warm light of moths
flying free.

New Year's Day in Prague

The silent mist whispers
across the Vltava and whitens
everything in its path
other than a dark ink-spot
of a lonely figure
on the St. Charles Bridge.

He sits on a small chair
in front of an easel
humbled by the silence
and becomes more like
the figures lining the bridge
with their angular features.

He paints gothic spires
rising like music
as does his brush
to the passion and insanity
of Liszt and Wagner
as statues

turn into ghosts
above the icy ribbon
of river disappearing
in the dying light
where geese are bound
in prayer.

Steven Pelcman

Nearby, the sun touches
each layered tombstone
of Jews like a fallen forest
but nothing is forgotten
when grass still grows
in ancient languages

and cradles the sweet air
and the dim light
of copper domes to almost
hear the mutterings of Mozart,
his arms raised like the wind
reliving the pain of genius.

The Waiting
(A painting by Degas)

Mother and daughter sit
on a narrow wooden bench
exchanging only silence.

We do not see
ballerina daughter's face
sprouting through

a cloud of chiffon
blue-bowed at the waist
as she rubs the impatience

of dance in her ankles
perched tight as a fist.

Mother is hunched in black
from hat to umbrella tip,
her wrists rest softly

against her knees bound
in sunlight, they shine
like Sunday's cross.

Settled in their bones they
wait as the aging of wood
comforted by shadows.

Steven Pelcman

A Cup of Tea

Winter brings a darkness
that her eyes cannot reach
and goes beyond what she remembers
when remembering is better forgotten

as her crooked fingers dip the
tea bag into steam
leaving her hands
with the smell of peppermint

and then she twirls
the string
that matches her veins
around the bag

so tightly that it leaves
her out of breath
as the sun dips
below her couch

to where a cat's furry sleep
welcomes the winter frost
as it too curls
into itself.

Old Man Walking to Market Place in Early Spring
(Halle, Germany 1997)

There is a little something left for him to do,
armed with a cane's brave wood tapping out the distance
alongside trams elbowing himself and struggling to breathe
between condemned buildings worn prison-grey,
occasionally mumbling, Guten Tag, until vegetables and fruit
are spread out before him and herds of other old people
flock with pigeons to share the warmth that color can give.

Steven Pelcman

Giverny
(For Monet)

An eyeful of yellow daisies
grow wild in bunches
just beyond the green shutters
of a kitchen full of copper pots
and pans hanging on the walls.

Here, in quiet solitude a burly
and bearded man had walked
across the dirt paths leading
to the bridge and the pond
of lily pads floating in the shadows.

He could walk all day, humbled
by the perfection he chased,
understanding the differences,
not in the colors chosen
of light and dark,

or of how time and space
change everything,
or even of how lines are measured out
but in where beginnings truly end
and where endings are only the beginning,

and discovering that imagination
is merely the moment understood.

Easter Spring Walk

It was a spring walk in April
they said; they being
veterans of country walks
made in spring or fall.

These walks are with older men
and women who carry baskets
of cheese and dark German bread
and flasks of schnapps and hot coffee.

They are locals who scout out
new walks to discover
every year in order to celebrate
the change of seasons;

and so we rose early
on a cold Easter morning
and marched past rail tracks and river bridges
and farms and into the countryside

as the trail cut through the vast
green landscape that distinguished itself
from the brown worn edges
of village buildings

until we arrived at a little church
seldom used and where a musty-ancient smell
still lingers and prayers can be imagined
as our echoed words gathered dust.

Steven Pelcman

The cold light entered
and discoloured through the
stain-glass windows
as we sat in unstable pews

pointing out the silver cross
and the ornaments
and the limp agony it protected
above the alter and podium

marked by a handprint
and the untouched outline of a bible
that must have found safe comfort
for so many years.

We rose and left
and from an outside narrow window
we glimpsed part of a coffin
kept in the basement

with a sword upon it
and was told it had belonged
to a knight from the holy wars
that had come home

to eternal rest
for a thousand years
in the glory of having saved
men's souls.

Mediation
(For K)

At the edge of a thick wood
on an outdoor porch
she designed space
with her body,
absorbing color and sound,
broken branches and struggling leaves

as sunlight
filled her with silence
and a trusting finch
drawn to the new shape of things
in search of forest sleep
flew to her arm.

And they became;
statuesque and wintry,
asleep and breathing out
their inner journeys of flight
to share heartbeats
and earthly warmth.

Cats

I have always wondered if
all cats are alike,
behave similarly
at night in crossing

a darkened street
in that country-dance frolic,
an uppity soldier's march
of spine and leg

that somehow slithers and
prances at the same time
with penetrating eyes
that musically glow

in fine sadness. I have stood
on a street abandoned and
waiting breathlessly
for the excursion between

car headlights. I have also
stood my ground on
the other side of the street,
an imaginary border crossing,

following every movement
till one slips by
up the curb and into
the deep shadows.

How proud
I was, how relieved
that I did not have
to go home with the agony

of guttural purring in my dreams
and reject the feather blanket comfort
into moulded warmth of the
woman beside me.

Steven Pelcman

A Tourist's Welcome
(Mexico)

It is dry and hot but when the figs
are ripe, a parrot's frenzy encircles
the huge Nacapul Banyan-like tree

and the women walk
softly like the breeze
that passes overhead.

Above are shadows of birds
knotted in flight over Banderas Bay
as palm trees lean

into the sudden darkness
sweeping the moon's rim
with the light of fingertips.

A young woman strolls
along the stucco walls
crowned in bougainvillea

looking down at the city
embracing the darkness,
her braided hair

dances along her neck
wildly as do the vines
in the midst of iguanas

burros and jungle cardboard huts
where hotels are diamonds
on fingers caressing the bay.

The scent of sweet bananas and papayas
fill the streets of headless chickens
and soldiers guarding banks.

Steven Pelcman

Florida Turkeys Running Wild

There was high drama
in the big pasture
this morning as the rafter
of turkeys came running

out of the woods
where our horses graze
and rushed to the tree
where the corn-feeder hangs

above the wet grass
and dried-up acorns.
The metallic glittering
of red, green and copper,

of bronze and gold
of the single male bird
was camouflaged by the drab
brownish colored hens

and their wild feathers
struggled to feed
in the horse's shadows.
A horse's curiosity

was more than
the male could stand
as he started to strut
and puff his chest out,

its tail flaring wildly
gobbling like a jealous husband
until the horses neighed
and retreated

forming a single line
of twittering animal flesh
in the rising sunlight
as if waiting to greet a VIP.

They stood there,
even when the turkeys
ran off towards the forest,
not understanding

how such small bundles
of feathers and outstretched necks
could cause such commotion
and unexpected fear.

Steven Pelcman

Fishing on the Galata Bridge
(Istanbul)

He had walked barefoot
with a pole on his shoulder
in the shadows

of the Mosque
reaching ahead of him;
a hand upon a hand

leading him to the bridge
over the Bosporus
where he must have thought

what it must be
to be a fish
only men take from the sea.

Silky twine is cast
as a warning shot
across the bow

in search of flapping gills
in the remaining pockets
of sunlight

where the last daily prayer
floats above the silent
movement beneath the darkness.

The skeletal pattern of
poles and lines and hooks
from atop the bridge

in the silhouettes of minarets
and glossy swagger
of fish evading moonlight

does not prevent
little boys running by
counting the fins

hanging over the pails
of water or women
in burqas

passing by dauntingly
not looking at
what they cannot see.

Steven Pelcman

Remembering Marrakech

They had fallen in love in the dim light
of the narrow alleyways clinging to her skin
and of souks shadowed by woollen rugs
hanging above stacked water-pipes.

They laughed amongst the bubbled glass
and wooden instruments vibrating
to the burning incense beating African sounds
against the red-stone walls for over 1000 years.

Vats of ink are stirred
and story tellers and street dentists
drift through the old Medina in the spiced air
where snake charmers, toothless, aside

the red-pink-baked low buildings
echo with the calls to prayer.
Prayers are swallowed by the ice-capped
Atlas peaks towering overhead and spreading

to the Sahara below as magicians
and mystics and monkey trainers
encircle them in the lantern light
to the rhythm of castanets

and lemon-grove air where palm tree breezes
and the scent of figs have stayed with him ever since.
Just beyond the reach of Marrakech
the train passes and pomegranates and olives

fill him with the memory of her turning him
back into the pilgrim he had once been.
His train lunges by flowering
a stream of black smoke

catching up to itself
leaving behind an endless sound
on sandy metal towards
a stark-white indifference.

It whizzes by a Berber's body rising as a mule
tosses its head forward and an old man
on a bicycle waving and children kicking
a soccer ball past the dark curves

of women's bodies balancing baskets
on their heads walking towards
a large tent flapping in the distance.
It passes a mangled herd of goats

roaming through the struggling dark faces
of young men huddling in circles
under the sun in night-blue smocks
praying in the sand.

Steven Pelcman

Sidewalk Bakery

The milky air of summer
swarms with bees
that carry them to a glass counter.

Full of warm bread
and cakes they swirl over
rumbling their bodies against

glass and cinnamon mired
in the honey and raisins
they mount and thread as if sky

or a lost cloud they marvel at
threatening the daylight
with a different blackness

unlike their own,
fluttering among the glazed
tops of sweetened dough

and it is a bond
they can return to,
a crazy love

of sunlight that stings
against glass
aimlessly as lovers often do

but they are not alone
for the old, poor man
who sits outside

at a wobbly table
with coffee and cigarette
in hand,

a shaking hand,
smells the honey
and warm bread

stares at the counter
with what can only be
sexual desire,

some hidden jealousy
of bees he imagines
he could have been.

Steven Pelcman

Lorelei
(German song played after
World War II Allied night raid, October 1943)

How thin the air is
for it to carry
the shallow breaths
of men darkened by evil.

They move out
of the smoky dust
with legs like twigs
shackled at the ankles,

protruding like beetles
circling within themselves;
their stubby movements,
inch forward from atop the hill.

Pain knows no tears
and the darkness
is lit by only the red heat
of cigarettes and a Kapo's grim face.

Marching downward,
they shift their weight
to the accompanying music
of violins leading them

to shelled-out craters,
to the burnt hulk
of disfigured metal,
hollow train cars

illuminated in flames
that scorch their flesh
as they drag out and rescue
slumbering bombs;

"Sleeping iron babies."

Smoke billows,
clings to their striped uniforms,
to their hard-shell faces
ignorant of sunlight.

There is little difference
between prisoner and guard
in the unknown limbs tossed aside
into the bonfires in the early light of dawn.

Steven Pelcman

A Quiet, Lonely Room for Dying

The contrast of light and dark
is never greater
than when you live
in a household for the dying,

who you find trapped
in a room you walk
in and out of
and yet the journey

of death can be so exotic
for the giving is absolute
and the evolution of little things
that is the politics of relationships

give way
to the smallness of our lives
in the lonely moments
of pampering and coddling.

With each fish movement
as if pressed against aquarium glass,
he mouths speechless words
you cannot understand

but you feel the distance
of his privacy
so separate from every other
moment outside his room

and you realize
you have known death
through media consumption
in the largeness of war

or in the little faces
of a child's starvation
or in the thrown away news stories
of a fast food manager's slain body

and garbage cans stuffed
with unwanted births
and sound bites of disease outbreaks
and the exodus of war victims

but a private death
should not be forgotten
as the slow passing of time
of generation to generation

family to family
person to person
is to be found
in a quiet, lonely room.

Steven Pelcman

Concentration Camp Number 144988
(For Dad)

Walls are decorated
with the tapestry of
family lives in pictures
that mark milestones

for him to remember
what he can
at 85 and dying
in a room of vulnerabilities.

Bald, his face sunken
and pear shaped,
narrow eyes sensitive to light
his frail body,

religious to the touch,
is immobile under
tumbled white sheets
yet he still manages to pucker

his lips and kiss my cheek
and more than ever before
the tattooed blue number
on his left arm,

once unnoticed, hidden
by the fullness of life
is stark and bold,
brave beyond its years

as if rising from the ashes
of burning ovens
stuffed with the charred limbs

of other families
reminding us that survival
has been a life long journey.

Steven Pelcman

The Last Train to Auschwitz

He stood by the wired fence which was
close enough to hear the train whistle
as shadows formed around his bent back

but all he could see were the moving stars
of yellow light pinned on the chests of dark figures
trudging down the dirt path

towards the smoke rising above the trees
and all he could hear was the shuffling
of feet but he could distinguish the differences

of men and women and the children that had just arrived
on the last train to Auschwitz and he was able to separate
the smells from the wet wooden barracks.

They passed by slowly having emptied out of
the cattle cars carrying a soiled warmth with them
as if violating the winter air that attacked his body

creeping alongside his protruding ribs and leaving him
with a hunger for more than the bites of stale bread
and cup of dirty soup he endured daily.

He watched with the trees from the distance sharing
the same darkness, the same breaths, knowing the silence,
knowing the slow march of shadows and the loneliness of waiting.

He had just finished his job and had held tightly,
the two gold teeth that were under the remaining ashes
of bones and shredded skin, in his fist and that

he could be gassed for this crime but he also knew
the guards would trade for gold, for any part of a Jew
that was worth smelling the gas in the freezing cold.

So he stood next to the fence with red knuckles and gold teeth
in his fist as the shuffling sounds grew faint and the smoke
thickened until the darkness became bigger and he was alone.

Steven Pelcman

A Father's Last Seven Days

Condemned to a world
of no context
he is only a memory
held by others

and in his last seven days
hospice nurses sat on a couch
and watched, waited, calculated
while he breathed in oxygen

and tasted only the salt
of tears on his lips.
For seven days
we stroked his bald head

caressed his arms and shoulders
told him the day and time
shaved him
and let him know

how grateful we were
for his love and hard work
and sacrifices
and although his body,

no longer his,
reduced to the technology of will,
the upheaval of God
beckoning him

in the sputtering convulsions
as every last drop
of air and strength he had
surged through him

without food or water,
he thrived on remaining shards
of thought and memory.
For seven days

we listened to the moans
and knew he was remembering
what he could not express, the moans
of his mother and sister

the tears that fell across his cheek
watching their stooped walk,
their backs framed in dark shadows
to the ovens down the dirt path.

For seven days the shadows
of the room spread across his body
making him whole again,
giving him some sense of peace.

We sat and walked
in vigil, waiting, hoping
he would think of only himself
and let go

Steven Pelcman

and for seven days
we loved him again
as all children learn to love
with the beauty

of a child's first and only truth
and playful touch
without the world
and life getting in the way.

Anne Frank Speaks

Do not weep for the faceless
are beyond thinking
of their daily work
standing like skinless trees
swaying black against the sun
swinging me beside the moist earth

on top of still-moving flesh
and then shovels
turning, turning
among the jigsaw pieces of torn skin
and bleached bones,
some eaten away

in the midst of their waste,
yet for those that survive
it is good to know
that daughters and sons
can be born from the agony
of golden teeth pulled from the dead.

But do not weep for me
for I am proud to have grown
into this discipline
and in truth
it was not an unknown darkness
that I joined

Steven Pelcman

but a familiar belonging
as I slipped next to Margot
and felt the memory of her face
and though the earth swallowed us
sound runs deep
and there are shared voices in the dark.

Do not weep
even though you knew
the end
from the very beginning.
this is not such an uncommon experience
after all

an argument can end in hatred
a kiss, in love
and though I did not believe at first,
I found God
and though I did not live
you found me.

Looking Down While Walking

What mirrors there
between the cracks
of cement, if not

a shrouded image
oozing from my skin
and the whispers

and giggles held firm,
the secrets lying flat
against the earth

collected amongst
the cigarette butts
and wind-tossed

wrappers and gum
with the empty promises
I have kept to myself.

They die a city street death
of the endless trampling
of everyone I do not know

and the movement of strangers
reborn within me. Each time
I pass this way,

each face that does not see mine,
each sound disconnected
to make a whole,

Steven Pelcman

each day a collection
of minutes upon cement,
an assortment of memories

in the eyes fused together
looking back up at every person
passing by.

Are memories removed
for the dead and replaced
by the newly born? I wonder

who sees me now
on this wintry street
with lamppost lights gleaming.

Waiting at Night

He has left again but she is accustomed
to the dark and listens to the uproar
of wind against the room
making shackled sounds
of prisoners running for freedom

running in the awkward darkness
when garbage cans fall
and trees so alike animals
spread their wings
rise and devour the darkness.

The wind reminds her
of the crying struggle of
a baby's first cry
or a man's last breath
beating against the blackness.

The window is ajar
with cold air flushing through
and filling her body with
the memory of wild leaves
gasping for air

making her eyes grope
for the tiny pockets of light
a shadow makes when it passes
the emptiness and is smothered
by the oncoming daylight.

Steven Pelcman

It is not the wind or the darkness
or the loneliness or sudden sounds
that strike fear or even of the chill
that creeps inside of her and then warms
her skin but it is the waiting, she minds most.

A Proper Place

He has taught me to save
the last breath for myself

for there is a language spoken
in the dark I do not yet know

but can hear in the weeds
beside a tombstone in this city

of graves as waves of light
erase almost everything

but the freshly placed flowers
where I imagine

my father's hands
are sure to be.

Steven Pelcman

A Mother's Final Journey

When the sun lowers its head
into turbulent clouds
rooftops of nearby buildings
begin to unravel their true color

as my mother walks out onto
the narrow catwalk like a prowler
uncomfortable in the dark.
Her cheeks, tinged red

and scarred by shadows
form black pools inching
closer and closer
as the wind curls her scarf

around her neck so that she begins
to tear leaving a trail of light
she has always better understood
in the darkness.

The empty apartment windows
sense the separation and rattle
as they absorb the end of day
when she descends the staircase

to start the ritual exercise-march
through the parking lot dividing buildings
under the watchful eyes of a quarter moon
and the drawn windows of spectators

aging in their wheelchairs and walkers
accompanied by their Haitian care-takers
standing against the railings and wishing they
could be like her.

She looks down forcing her way
forward past license plates of places
she no longer remembers and into
the soundless air thinking

of what has brought her to this
knowing it is much too late
to die young, knowing she will return
to an apartment and ask forgiveness

of the peeling paint and torn window screens
of the back porch, sit and drift away
into the peaceful melodies of song birds
waiting for even the moon to escape.

Steven Pelcman

A Father Leaving
(Poland 1940)

The soft light that slowly
chisels her father's face
etched in rough lines
and sunken eyes

fades in the oncoming darkness,
as he prepares to pack the horse
and wagon with goods to sell,
and it makes it hard for him

to let her go
watching her stand
in the shadows
of a pale moon.

He wonders if all little girls
think of their fathers as heroes
and if the silence of his leaving
will whisper through her

and she feels the reins
beat against her own skin
as his slumped image
on the wagon seat

pounds into her chest
and forever the cold and frost
will be spiced by this memory
of wheels circling away.

If she could she would lift
the darkness overhead and twirl
under a sky laden with the deep
sound of his voice

but instead she watches the dark
keep to itself and the trees struggle
to hold onto the dying light
so she stays in her room

learning to measure time
on what she can depend on
understanding that light
has the same order as tears

or music or wax creeping down the sides
of a candle burning itself back
to itself with a purpose
she can understand.

She knows that she is almost envious
of an animal so well trusted
or of the children
that will play with the snow

like candy while running after the wagon
and jumping in the muddied horse footprints
and over the piles of manure that some
will remember him by

and she also knows that the young
are being taken away, shot
and their bodies wrapped in linen
and prepared like young trees

Steven Pelcman

wound tightly and transferred
to some other hole
in the ground to sleep and dream
beneath the stars of a Polish winter.

Her body is a battlefield
of pain not knowing if
she will ever see
her father again

and from her window
flaky and smouldering ash
rise from the blackened bibles
and the wooden pews

of an oven-burning synagogue
where the dangling-gutted- body
and legs twirling in the dead air
of a man hanging for being a Jew

nobody can hear
or see how much darkness
a building on fire
can claim for its own.

Madrid

Outside of the Prado museum
the old lady, alone and
in a long black-woolen coat,

her hand open to the wave
of pigeons gathering
and answering a prayer making

her smile and mimic the sounds of flight
offers benediction with the bread crumbs
she tosses for the salvation she seeks.

Across the way on the side
of the Prado the free entry line
attracts Japanese students, a bag-lady

and I watching the sun sliding
down on the full length
leather coat on the man in front of us.

The evening street lamps
turn on as rattling leaves
compete with the chatter

and wind blowing January
through the growing line
of people waiting to go in.

Who among us
could have sat
in repose as a gift

Steven Pelcman

to the artist's hand,
to nurture and guide
his eyes and thoughts

and wander among us
digging deep into
our very souls?

The poor artist would never
know the betrayal or
hear the silence of our footsteps.

Hailfingen-Tailfingen 1944-45
(Concentration labor-camp workers outside Stuttgart,
Germany building an airfield runway)

Blades of summer grass
grow tall and thin
in the half-shadows
and are used to the movement

of their empty bodies,
diseased and hobbled,
dragging across the hidden fields
like sick animals.

They shuffle towards the quarry
to load up the stones to build
the runway young German boys
will take off from.

Their shadows no larger
than the tallest weeds
walk behind wheelbarrows
and cows meandering,

past villagers on bicycles and
under the flak that smudges
the perfect sky
so that the Night Fighters

they claw their way across
the dried earth for, could bomb
and kill beneath the stars.
These Auschwitz outcasts

Steven Pelcman

who had escaped the ovens
were boys themselves having left
their mothers and fathers in the piles
of ash their train had taken them from

and across the German countryside
of burnt out buildings and lost souls
of men retreating to the rubble
spread out in every direction.

The young flyers rubbed dirt into their hands
for luck; the same dirt the Jews and prisoners
filled in the mass grave of men
bundled like bales of hay.

Toulouse

Poor Henri's slumped shoulder
and bulging back shifted
to the weight of a women

walking past his table,
her broad back winged
in black and her narrowed

tern legs pirouetting
the colorful undergarment
as loud as laughter

so that when she turned
on the dance floor
he was hidden from the light

and he would have told you
it was meant to be
because darkness could not be

protected for it to be understood
it needed to be ugly
so that it could be beautiful

in the imperfections he drew
so perfectly. This is what the little man
understood best

Steven Pelcman

shielded by a dark moustache and beard
his spectacles sliding down
the angle of his cane

as his brittle hips made him awkward
enough for him to be tolerated
and unafraid.

The World Beneath

When the wind ceases
to blow, these tired hills
forgive the darkness
its cowardice,

having turned its back
more than once
to silently pray
for forgiveness;

for the earth
to stop turning
and turning,
and pretend that god

still lives among us.
From beyond my window
I know there are rats
licking their wounds,

small birds disintegrating,
ants forming lines
among the crawling
twitching threads of light

and the city buildings
tucked beneath and between
the blades of grass
never ending.

Steven Pelcman

The night is still;
it is always still
at some point,
except for the movement

and voices we do not see,
do not hear,
the tiny breaths we cannot
measure, the little shadows

against pebbles and ant hills,
the fallen twigs and dying leaves,
the piles of shit and broken bottles
and the muddy paths, endless and alone.

Between the wood and bark
the forest grows deeper, darker
more alive with a constant chattering
on bended branch and gurgling gulps

of rain water and the slithering swish
through the grassy air protected by the
spider mazes growing wider and larger
webbed between plush green yearnings.

Here, there is strength beyond its capacity,
a world of acceptance we cannot emulate,
a living and dying breeding ground
that will not pass judgment when we are gone.

A Giraffe Surprises Us
(South Africa)

It muscles its way
out of the woods
and the jeep screeches
as we shift forward
in our seats listening
to its metallic bone sounds
on a narrow hard-mud path
through the jungle bush.

With no room to pass
it jerks along,
ahead of us,
dark-brown patches bouncing
and a tail signalling
it will do as it pleases.

It speeds up,
gallops,
we drive faster
and follow the breath
of its neck
to the hippo pool

until the giraffe
fumbles and slips
to its side,
turns to strike
but is distracted by
overgrown leaves
giving shade to the road.

Steven Pelcman

And we sit anxiously,
while its jaws munch
and saliva falls
in feathered-dusk light
and hippo moans
burst through burlap-water
full of eyes and gaping mouths.

The giraffe lets us
tiptoe to the water
lined with crocodiles

and from across
the lily-covered
banks of the Banzi pan
full of teeth,

drums beat out
smoky sounds
rising above
green-barked fever trees
swaying beneath the moon.

Spring

After a long winter
spring begins in a whisper
of daffodils and tulips
rising out of a cool haze
above the frozen short grass.

Rabbits sniff and scoot
across a hillside's quiet
humming of bees buried
in soil awakening the queen
from her lonely sleep.

The earth moves slowly,
and in a new light
a stranger inside escapes
into a memory of seeded air
and the feathery voices

of goldfinches turning
lemon-yellow and wrens
gathering straw to nest
or robins digging for worms;
all bursting into song.

The woodland floor trembles
in the long-awaited sigh and is
reborn to a chorus of water rising
in the scent of herbs and the
early-morning flight north of birds.

Steven Pelcman

Somewhere a black bear exhales
and moans and wanders out
of the darkness through a ravine
of boulders and fallen tree limbs
to feed on the carcass of winter's folly.

The earth's tilt moves us
closer to the light
when new-born cry
and when we step away
from our own shadows.

Every Season

Born of yellow
when the blue air is warm
and birds are unafraid
to swoop over the green grass

when your children would roll
across a steady stream of ants
unnoticed and starting to
build a shelter

and squirrels make
a sudden appearance
from behind the bark
of trees gasping for breath.

Winter falls in a downpour
of darkness when everything
loses its curves and circles
and resumes straight lines,

when grave-sites
are most lonely
and laughter is caught
between white walls.

In a lingering moment
of pinks and purples, you look up
and listen for the sound of flowers
rising and shadows withdrawing.

Steven Pelcman

Every season you open
a black book and erase
the names and phone numbers
you no longer need to remember

and neatly remove pictures
from their frames
and stuff them under plastic.
It is a routine relived

each season in silence,
when words have been
repeated so many times before
that you know them by heart.

Keystone Cowboy

Just below the face of Mt. Rushmore
where presidents perch out into the setting sun
and nest in the rocky beds of stone
Keystone sits below like a disappointed lover.

The tourists flock so that children
wearing two-gun holsters and cowboy hats
tugging at their father's sides can stand beside
an old man dressed in cowboy regalia.

His tired smile and long whiskers
half scare the children who are staring at his
silver handle guns and cowboy boots and
buckskin leather-yellowed jacket one size too large.

He shuffles and buckles in the wind
as a proud father takes pictures while
a wife stands by with hands on her hips
and a blank stare on her face.

He must have been 90 having lived in Keystone
when Carrie Ingalls had lived there just before he
had ridden across Texas and then a part of the Panhandle
till deciding to ride horseback to South Dakota.

He had been a Texas Ranger then an actor in
silent films reliving the old Dime novels
of the exploits of bad men and gunfighters,
Sheriffs and legends born on the flimsy

Steven Pelcman

paper of a publisher spreading the glory
of the American west from an office in New York
or Chicago or anywhere legends go to die. The old man
put his hand out for small change as the father walked away

with his two children who had stared at the old man
but could not see the last buffalo grazing in a meadow,
eagles circling in the sunset, the trail full of steers
edging their way across the flats towards a river rising

on its banks or the swinging doors of a saloon and
the lonesome cowboy coming off the range full of dust
and sweat. They could not look inside of him to see
a prairie storm cutting and burning across the land

or a lone Indian sitting atop a hill
as the train burning wood and coal
left its mark in the sky. They could not feel
the wind at their backs on a horse too strong,

too fast headed to some forgotten gold camp, or
lighting a fire in a half-torn shanty full of dead birds
and wild dogs. They could not know the smell of buckskin
leather and the empty streets of Keystone.

Three Graves

The ranch house roof
weighed down by snowdrifts
peeked out from the shelter
of forest shadows
surrounding a frozen meadow.

Footprints leading from the
house to three small brown
wooden crosses tied with horsehair
was the only color alive
for as far as your eyes could see.

In the corral, to the side of
the house stood Betsy,
an old mare who leaned against
the aged timber wagging its tail
in the clouded air.

The shovel old Jim
had used to bury
the children remained
straight-up in the snow
leaving its thin shadow

to hold any warmth
possible in the late winter
of '73 when smallpox
spread from family
to family.

Steven Pelcman

They say his wife walked
out of the house the night the
last child died, walked straight
into the darkness, through the snow
and into the high hills.

She was naked and bloodied
and passed the graves singing
lullabies, prancing and then running
into the barren timber never to be heard of
or seen again.

When a neighbor who had
trekked three miles in glassy sunlight
on snowshoes made of cow-guts and saddle
rope and sawed-off fire logs to see if Old Jim
was still alive, he found the house burned down

Betsy gone and a different toy for each child
sitting in front of each grave. He found Jim
swinging from a deadened tree out back
whose limbs almost reached the ground
with his long body swaying freely.

The neighbor said, as the story goes,
that Jim swaying was the only sign of life
he could feel. Other than that, there was only
silence except for the wind passing as if voices
singing lullabies.

A Sad Tune

The little girl
clutched at her mother's torn dress
trying to keep up as the slave master
smiled wide at her fumbling legs

in the pouring rain.
The ankle bracelets made her
ankles swollen into clumpy
knobs of skin bleeding down

her legs as an old "darkie" sang
and the owner on horseback
riding proudly as if he had written
the sad tune.

The black shuffling line mostly
of young men, their muscled backs
struggling to keep afoot, to not lose
hold of the man before them in line.

This chorus of beaten flesh heading to the cotton
fields, pass the old house towering
above them, with its circular front porch
and little girls giggling into their iced tea.

About the Author

Steven Pelcman is an American educator, film producer and published author who has been residing in Germany for over 19 years. He has a history of having worked in Hollywood as a producer and reader analyst who was also involved in a magazine entertainment program as Executive producer, titled, Yesterdays, a development project which also led him to Washington DC and an invitation to President George H. Bush's inauguration and recognition in the field of TV family programming. Prior to relocating to Germany, Mr. Pelcman, originally from the Bronx, NY had also lived in New Orleans and Los Angeles. He graduated Rockland Community College where he received his AA Degree and SUNY New Paltz where he studied English and literature and graduated in 1976. Mr. Pelcman is now single and his children reside in California.

In Germany, Mr. Pelcman founded a private school, ELT, focusing on teaching English language skills and eventually this led to a partnership with Siemens throughout Germany. He continues to teach and consult regarding communication skills at the University of Education in Karlsruhe, Germany and at the Cooperative State University in Karlsruhe, Germany and for many schools and corporations in southern Germany. He continues to publish and as recently as 2013, he produced a short film titled, Sugar, based on his own work.

Mr. Pelcman's poetry and short stories have been published in many magazines and journals including: *The Windsor Review, The Innisfree Poetry Journal, Fourth River magazine, River Oak Review, Poetry Salzburg Review, Tulane Review, The Baltimore Review, The Warwick Review, The Cape Rock magazine, The Greensboro Review, Iodine Poetry Journal, Rockhurst Review magazine* and many others. He was nominated for the 2012 and 2017 Pushcart Prizes. His first volume of poetry titled, **like water to STONE** was released in the fall of 2017 by Adelaide Books Publishers from New York. **American Voices** poetry book published by Outlaws Publishing 2017. **Where the Leaves Darken** by Adelaide Books is Mr. Pelcman's third volume of poetry.

Steven Pelcman continues to travel the world, write, publish and teach in an effort to reach readers and share universal experiences, to prepare students of which many will become future teachers and travel to interact with many cultures.

Steven Pelcman says that "Capturing the voices of humor or pain, making the small moments epic and witnessing the trials and tribulations of the human experience which captures the heart and mind is what drives the work."
http://stevenpelcman.blogspot.de

The author wishes to thank the following publications

The Waiting, In New Orleans an Old Black Man Tells You about the South,

Notes from Eastern Germany

- *Paris Atlantic* magazine USA/France

A Hospital Vie

- *Down in the Dirt Magazine* USA

Meditation, Concentration Camp Number 144988,

Anne Frank Speaks

- *Nomad's Choir* magazine USA

Easter Spring Walk

- *The Faircloth Review*

Keystone Cowboy,

Three Graves,

A Sad Tune

courtesy of *Outlaws Publishing/American Voices*

www.ingramcontent.com/pod-product-compliance
Lightning Source LLC
Chambersburg PA
CBHW060457080526
44584CB00015B/1453